# THE UK NINJA FOODI COOKBOOK 2023

APPROVED

## By: Judi Clark

# TABLE OF CONTENTS

## BREAKFAST RECIPES

# TABLE OF CONTENTS

## POULTRY RECIPES

# TABLE OF CONTENTS

## MEAT RECIPES

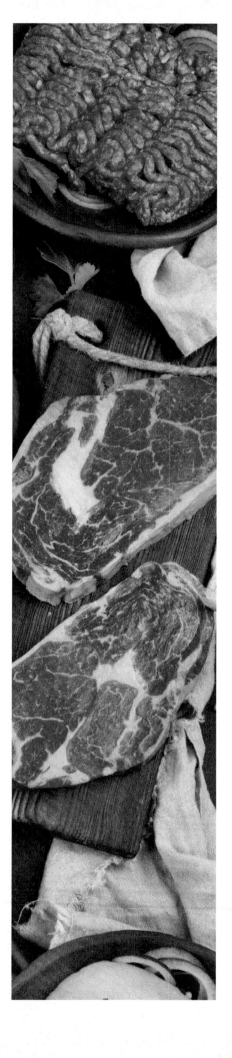

# TABLE OF CONTENTS

## SIDE RECIPES

# TABLE OF CONTENTS

## FISH AND SEAFOOD

# TABLE OF CONTENTS

## DESSERT RECIPES

# BREAKFAST

# Marzipan EASTER TREAT

## Ingredients

- 50g of dried apricots
- A 42g cube of yeast
- 370g flour
- 50g marzipan
- 3g of salt
- 65g melted butter
- egg yolk
- 175ml milk
- One egg
- 30g sugar

## Directions

1. In the beginning, preheat the milk in the microwave lukewarm, then add sugar & yeast to the milk and dissolve the yeast.
2. Transfer the flour to a wide bowl and crack the egg on it, add salt & melted butter.
3. Then add the milk mixture to the flour bowl. Knead the whole mix well until you make a smooth dough.
4. Cut the marzipan & apricots into little slices, and add and knead them in the prepared dough to combine.
5. Let the dough rise in a warm environment for about thirty to forty-five mins.
6. When the dough is raised, knead it again and separate it into three pieces. Roll out longer three strands of them.
7. Place three ends on top of each other and alternately add the strands over each other, making a braided braid. Link both ends together to form a wreath.
8. Transfer the wreath to a small cake tin that will match your ninja foodi. Prepare your machine. Insert the low feed grid into your machine's pot. Put the yeast braid on it. Leave it for about ten to fifteen mins.
9. Brush the braid with beaten egg yolk, and add some sugar over. Seal the lid and set the unit to the BAKE function, at 175ºC and start cooking.
10. After thirty mins, cover the braid with aluminium foil to make sure that it will not become too brown.
11. After about forty to forty-five minutes, check with a Chopstick if there is still dough on the chopstick, and cook for a further five to ten minutes. Serve it warm!

### Cooking & Prep Time: 45 mins

#### Servings: 4

1

# LENTIL RAGU

## Ingredients

- A rinsed and drained tin of green lentils
- 300g gluten free tagliatelle
- 15ml of garlic-infused olive oil
- A peeled large carrot
- A chopped tin of tomatoes
- One onion, chopped
- A pot of vegetable stock
- A tsp of paprika
- A tsp of mixed herbs
- A half cup of cranberry juice
- A stalk celery
- Salt & pepper

## Directions

1. Set your Ninja Foodi to the sear/sauté cooking mode on medium heat, pour the oil and, finely chop carrot & celery, and add them along with the chopped onion. Sauté for five mins.
2. Add the tomatoes, stock, paprika, lentils, herbs and cranberry juice, stir the components together, Close the lid, Choose the Slow Cook mode on high, set the timer for four hours, and Press START/STOP to start.
3. After the cooking process is completed, open the vent and allow the pin to drop before opening the lid, add salt & pepper to taste.
4. Prepare the tagliatelle following the mentioned instructions in the packet. combine this cooked tagliatelle with the ragu and serve.

Cooking & Prep Time: 4 hrs 10 mins

Servings: 4

# BREAKFAST OAT COOKIES

## Ingredients

- 25g Dark chocolate chips
- 50g salted peanut butter, smooth
- 200g apple puree, unsweetened
- 35g cranberries, dried
- 110g porridge oats, gluten-free

## Directions

1. In the beginning, Use baking paper to line the air fry basket of your Ninja Foodi Unit.
2. Next, combine all the listed components in your blender and mix to until you make dough.
3. Form six equal balls out of the dough, and press them down to get your desired form of cookies.
4. Place the cookies in the prepared basket, put the basket into the Unit and set it to the "BAKE/ROAST" function.
5. Cook for twelve mins at 180ºC.
6. After the cooking process of the cookies is done, keep them on the baking paper to cool down so you guarantee a smooth removal. Serve them cold!

Cooking & Prep Time: 30 mins

Servings: 2

3

# AVOCADO EGGS HALVES

## Ingredients

- Two slices of sourdough bread
- Pepper & sea salt
- Two large eggs
- A halved large ripe avocado, pit removed

## Directions

1. Put the reversible rack in the pot of the Ninja unit, the rack should be in the higher position. Seal the crisping lid. choose GRILL and preheat it for five mins.
2. Then, add the sourdough bread slices to the rack, and always on GRILL cooking function, set the time to four mins. Turn the bread halfway through. Transfer to plates.
3. Scoop out a portion of the avocado halves where the pit was, making wells deep enough for the eggs.
4. Grease the toast with this scooped-out avocado flesh if you want or just discard it. Season with salt and pepper.
5. Put those halves on aluminium with the foil flesh side up, and put them on the rack in the pot, the rack should be in the lower position, then crack one egg into each avocado half and season with salt & pepper.
6. Close the crisping lid. Choose ROAST, at 190ºC, and set the time to ten mins. Press START/STOP to start. Serve them along with the toast.

### Cooking & Prep Time: 20 mins

Servings: 2

4

# EESY CORNBREAD

## redients

- g polenta
- g of baking powder
- 0ml vegetable oil
- 0g of Sea salt
- A medium egg
- 250ml whole milk
- 125g grated cheddar cheese
- Cooking spray
- 20g granulated sugar

## Directions

1. In the first step, Put the Multi-Purpose Pan in the pot of the unit. Seal the crisping lid. Choose the GRILL cooking function, set the time to ten mins, and press START/STOP to start preheating.
2. Mix the flour with sugar, polenta baking powder, and salt in a mixing bowl, then add milk, egg, and oil to the dry components and whisk well to combine.
3. Add cheese and stir to incorporate with the mixture.
4. After the Ninja Foodi & pan have been preheated, unlock the lid, and use the cooking spray to spray the pan.
5. Transfer the blend you've made to the prepared pan, Seal the crisping lid. Choose the BAKE/ROAST cooking mode, 180ºC, and set the time to twenty-five mins. Press START/STOP to start.
6. Cook until a wooden toothpick inserted into the centre comes out clean.
7. After the cooking process is completed, pull the rack & the pan out of the unit and put the pan in a cooling rack for five mins before serving.

### Cooking & Prep Time: 30 mins

Servings: 8

6

# TURKISH EGGS BREAKFAS

## Ingredients

- Two minced garlic cloves
- 15ml of cider
- 300g Yoghurt
- 5ml of olive oil
- Four eggs
- Salt & pepper & Toasted bread for serving
- A tsp of chopped mint
- Two tbsp chopped dill + some for serving
- To prepare the warm butter:
- A Pinch of chilli flakes, paprika, and cumin
- Two tbsp of melted butter

## Directions

1. After turning on the Ninja Foodi unit, choose the slow-cook mode (High), then pour 1500ml water with the two tbsp of cider into the pot, start the timer and let the mixture heat up for around ten to fifteen minutes. Meanwhile, crack the eggs into separate small bowls and leave them aside.
2. When it's completed, open the lid and use a spoon to make a whirlpool in the water, and then add the cracked eggs successively, Seal and let it cook for around seven to eight minutes.
3. At the same time, combine the rest of the listed ingredients in a medium bowl except those in "the warm butter" section, add some salt and pepper to season and divide the mixture between two separate bowls.
4. Next, mix the components mentioned in "the warm butter" part together, season, and keep warm.
5. When eggs are cooked, add them to the yoghurt mixture and pour some of the warm butter on top, Serve with warm bread after garnishing with some dill if you like too!

### Cooking & Prep Time: 15 mins

Servings: 2

5

# POTATO HASH

## Ingredients

**For the hash:**
- 1g of salt
- 450g peeled sweet potato, cubed
- Two garlic cloves, crushed
- 45ml of extra virgin olive oil
- 2g of smoked paprika
- Half tsp of cumin
- A white onion, diced
- Half tsp of ground turmeric

**For the guacamole:**
- One avocado, mashed
- 15g of diced tomato
- One chilli flakes pinch
- A drizzle of fresh lime juice
- 2g of diced white onion

**For the salsa:**
- 50g diced tomatoes
- 2g of diced white onion
- lime wedges
- 4g of diced fresh coriander

## Directions

1. In a bowl, mix the paprika, and 30ml oil with the potatoes, turmeric, salt, and cumin and toss.
2. Then, transfer to your Ninja Unit, Select Air Crisp mode and set the temp at 200°C, Cook for fifteen mins with a stir halfway through.
3. At the same time, heat up a pan with the remaining 15ml of oil over medium heat, then stir in the diced white onion (except two tbsp for the salsa & guacamole) and crushed garlic. keep cooking for about twelve mins and stir occasionally.
4. Mix the components listed in the "guacamole" part in a mixing bowl, and the components mentioned in the "salsa" part in a separate bowl.
5. After the cooking process of the potatoes is completed, transfer them to the cooked onion pan and stir to combine.
6. Transfer to serving platters, add the guacamole over them, top with salsa and squeeze lime. Serve!

## Cooking & Prep Time: 35 mins

### Servings: 2

# CRANBERRY OAT BARS

## Ingredients

- 100g whole cranberry sauce
- A cup of plain flour
- 100g porridge oats
- A half tsp of bicarbonate of soda
- 170g soft brown sugar
- A zested large orange
- 120g of chopped cold butter
- A tsp of ground cinnamon

## Directions

1. In the beginning, grease a 20cm cake tin using the butter, and line the base with baking parchment.
2. Combine oats with flour, sugar, orange zest, bicarbonate of soda, and cinnamon in a wide bowl.
3. Rub the butter in the oat mixture using your hands until it looks like rough breadcrumbs.
4. Add 1/2 of the oat combination into the lined cake tin and press onto the bottom.
5. Spread cranberry sauce over and spread the rest of the oat mix on top.
6. Insert the cake tin in the reversible rack, the rack should be in the lower position, and insert the rack into your Ninja Foodi pot.
7. Choose BAKE/ROAST at 170°C and set the time to thirty-five mins. Press START/STOP to start.
8. After twenty mins, check the browning and if it appears too much, add foil tightly over the cake tin. Then Check for doneness after thirty-five mins.
9. Remove the cake tin from the pot and allow it to cool down, slice and serve.

### Cooking & Prep Time: 50 mins

### Servings: 8

# SHAKSHOUKA

## Ingredients

- 400g cherry tomatoes tin
- 50g crumbled feta cheese
- One onion, thinly sliced
- A half tsp of dried thyme
- One red pepper, sliced
- 100g chorizo sausage, sliced
- 2g of paprika
- A tsp of cumin
- Four eggs
- A tsp of oregano
- Two garlic cloves, crushed
- A tsp of chilli flakes
- 15ml of oil
- Freshly chopped herbs
- Salt & pepper
- Bread for serving

## Directions

1. First, choose the sear/sauté mode on your Ninja Foodi and preheat it at medium heat for exactly five mins without sealing the lid.
2. Then, pour oil, add the onions & peppers and sauté for around two mins, then add garlic with sausage and cook for a further two mins to crisp up the sausage, add the spices, stir to combine, and cook for one min more.
3. Unlock the tin of cherry tomatoes and add it to the pot, add some water to the tin, stir and pour in too, and simmer for around four to five minutes to get a thickened sauce.
4. Make four medium holes in the sauce and add an egg in each hole, lock the lid and let the eggs poach for about five mins.
5. When It's completed, Place everything on serving platters, top with the cheese & herbs, and serve with crusty bread.

### Cooking & Prep Time: 30 mins

### Servings: 2

# TEA CAKE

## Ingredients

- 345g of your favourite Dried Fruit
- Two eggs beaten
- 200g Light Brown Sugar
- 300ml Indian tea cooled, Made of one Bag of Masala Chai
- 250g Self Raising Flour

## Directions

1. One day before, you will soak the fruit in a bowl with tea overnight.
2. Next, combine eggs, flour, fruit & sugar in a bowl and mix them well, then pour the mixture into a greased 20cm loose bottomed round tin.
3. Pour 350ml of water into your Ninja Foodi and place a trivet into it. Put the cake tin on top.
4. Close the lid and select Pressure on High. Seal the Pressure Valve and set the time to sixty mins. When it beeps, Release the compression naturally for ten mins. Enjoy!

Cooking & Prep Time: 13 mins

Servings: 8

10

# POULTRY

---

# CAJUN SPATCHCOCK CHICKEN

## Ingredients

- 1.8 kg of Chicken, skin on & Spatchcocked
- Olive Oil
- 75g of Butter
- A tsp of Dry Oregano
- A tsp and a half of Paprika
- Four large cloves of Garlic, crushed
- 15ml of lemon juice
- A half tsp of Cayenne Pepper
- Salt & Pepper

## Directions

1. In the beginning, after pat drying the chicken, season the inside and out with salt and pepper. Next, combine the Cayenne, Paprika, Oregano, Butter, Lemon Juice, Garlic and Salt & Pepper in a mixing bowl until they are combined.
2. Run the Ninja Foodi unit and set it on the Air Fry cooking mode, at 180°C. Set the time to ten mins and preheat.
3. While the unit is preheating, gently loosen the skin of the chicken. insert the butter under and over the skin until the crown is fully covered then season the Chicken & drizzle with olive oil.
4. Add the chicken to the Ninja Foodi and roast for ten mins breast side down.
5. Then rise the heat to 200°C, and roast for an additional twenty-five to thirty mins. Leave it for about ten mins to rest before serving.

Cooking & Prep Time: 1 hour

Servings: 4

# PEPPERED TURKEY ROULADES

## Ingredients

- Two turkey breasts
- Fresh herbs
- 90g cream
- 15g of mustard
- 200g cream cheese
- Four slices of beef bacon
- A garlic clove
- One tbsp of pickled green peppercorns
- Rice or Tagliatelle
- Paprika powder (sweet), pepper, salt
- 15 to 30ml of olive oil
- 90ml vegetable stock
- Sauce thickener

## Directions

1. In the first step, we will start by cutting the breasts into flat slices and then pounding them using a meat tenderiser till they become flat, Coat them with some of the cream cheese and season with pepper & salt. Roll each up to a roulade and fold around a slice of beef bacon on each.
2. Set the Unit to the Sear/Sauté cooking mode on medium. Pour the olive oil into the pot and roast the roulades on all sides. Slice the garlic thinly and add them.
3. Now, change the setting on the Ninja Foodi Unit to Bake/Roast at 190°C and set the time to twenty mins. Lock the lid and press START/STOP to begin.
4. During the cooking time, in a bowl, mix the rest of the cream cheese with the cream, stock, and mustard. Season with paprika powder, salt & pepper.
5. Ten to fifteen before the cooking time end, open the lid and add the cream mix.
6. When it's completed, transfer the roulades to a serving plate, add the fresh herbs over and serve with noodles if you like.

### Cooking & Prep Time: 40 mins

### Servings: 4

# TASTY FENUGREEK CHICKEN

## Ingredients

**For the marinade:**
- 900g of Chicken Thighs
- 8g of Salt
- 100g Plain Yoghurt
- A tsp of Red Chilli Powder
- One and a half tsp of Coriander Powder
- Two tsp of Garam Masala

**For the curry:**
- Two Bay Leaves
- A tsp of Cumin Seeds
- 45ml of Oil
- 2cm Cinnamon Sticks
- 3/4 tbsp of Ginger Paste
- Four Cloves of Garlic, crushed
- A pierced Green Chilli
- Six Peppercorns
- 100ml Water
- A medium Onion, diced
- Salt
- A bunch of fresh Fenugreek Leaves
- 45g of Plain Yoghurt

## Directions

1. Mix all the ingredients listed in "the marinade" part in a wide bowl, then the chicken in and coat. Leave it to marinade for about twenty-five mins.
2. Run your Ninja Foodi machine, choose the Sauté cooking mode and heat up the oil on it, add cumin seeds, and after one min, start adding Ginger, Bay Leaves, Green Chilli, Cinnamon, Garlic and Peppercorns. After thirty seconds, add the Onions & Salt. Cook for about six to seven mins.
3. Now, add the Chicken & Fenugreek and cook for two mins. Then pour water over and stir. Close the lid and set the vent to seal. Select Pressure cook on high and set the time for around fifteen mins.
4. When it's over, let the pressure release naturally for ten mins, and then shift the vent to release steam. Unlock the lid and choose Saute. add the Yoghurt and cook for an additional five mins. Then check and adjust the seasoning as you desire. Serve!

### Cooking & Prep Time: 40 mins

Servings: 6

# NINJA FOODI TURKEY CROWN

## Ingredients

- 2kg of turkey crown
- 15ml of runny honey
- One orange, sliced
- Sprigs of thyme
- Eight to ten pancetta slices
- A small onion, peeled & quartered
- 250ml water
- Two bay leaves
- Salt & pepper
- 15ml of oil

## Directions

1. Loosen the skin over the breast. Put two orange slices, a thyme sprig, and a bay leaf under the skin, on both breast sides, and crisscross pancetta slices over the duck breast. Season to taste.
2. Inside the pot of the Ninja Foodi Unit, pour water and add onions, Add the rack inside, and put the prepared turkey crown on it.
3. Lock the pressure lid, (the valve in the SEAL). Set the Unit to the PRESSURE cooking mode on Hight, and set the time to twenty-five mins. Press START/STOP to start. At the same time, whisk honey with oil in a little bowl.
4. When the cooking time is done, shift the valve to the VENT position to quick release the pressure.
5. Brush the turkey with the honey mixture. Lock the crisping lid, reset the Unit to the AIR CRISP cooking mode at 200ºC and set the time to ten mins. Press START/STOP to start.
6. After the 10 minutes are over, (The turkey will become golden brown and the intern temp is 75ºC) pull the cooked turkey out of the machine and give it a rest of fifteen mins covered in foil before serving.
7. Brush the turkey with the honey mixture. Lock the crisping lid again, choose AIR CRISP mode at 200ºC and set the time to ten mins. Press START/STOP to start.
8. Once it's done, (The turkey will become golden brown and the intern temp is 75ºC) pull the cooked turkey out of the unit and give it a rest of fifteen mins covered in foil before serving.

### Cooking & Prep Time: 50 mins

### Servings: 6

# AWESOME CHICKEN NUGGETS

## Ingredients

**For the batter:**
- An egg
- 90g Plain Flour
- A half cup of Water
- For the breadcrumbs:
- 1g of Paprika
- Half tsp of Garlic Powder
- 5g of salt
- Half tsp of Cayenne Pepper
- 110g Breadcrumbs

**For the chicken:**
- 30ml of Oil
- 900g cubed Chicken Breast

## Directions

1. In a bowl, mix the components listed in the "For the batter" part. Repeat the same operation with the components listed in the "For the breadcrumbs" section on a separate large platter.
2. Run the Ninja Foodi unit, add the basket into it, choose Air Fry mode, and preheat.
3. At the same time, dip the chicken pieces in the batter mix and coat them in breadcrumbs.
4. Grease the basket using oil and add the prepared chicken in a single layer, spray them with Oil, and luck the lid, always in the Air Fry option at 180°C. Cook for five mins and then flip the chicken pieces.
5. Spray again and cook for an additional three to four mins till the chicken becomes golden. Serve!

Cooking & Prep Time: 20 mins

Servings: 4

# DELICIOUS DUCK RECIPE

## Ingredients

- A whole duck (around 2300g)
- One carrot
- 500ml water
- One onion, peeled
- Two apples, cored and quartered
- Six peppercorns
- A tsp of paprika
- Two bay leaves
- A half tsp of caraway seeds
- 15ml of oil
- Salt & pepper

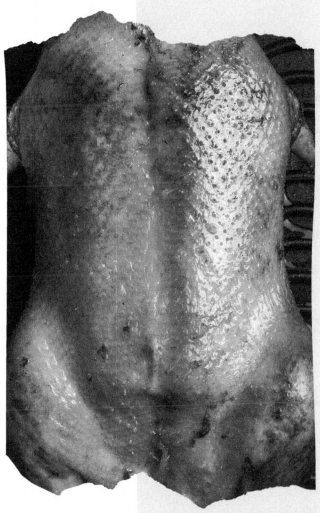

## Directions

1. As a first step, remove the packet of giblets and ends of wings from the duck. Rinse duck and tie legs together using cooking twine. Put it aside.
2. Now place all the listed components into the pot of your Ninja Foodi machine, insert the reversible rack in the lower position and put the prepared duck on it. Close the pressure lid, (the valve in the SEAL). Set the Unit on the PRESSURE cooking mode on Hight, and set the time to twenty mins. Press START/STOP to start.
3. During the cooking process, take a little bowl, add paprika, oil, salt & pepper and mix them together.
4. When the machine has completed the cooking time, set the valve to the VENT to quick release the pressure.
5. Open the lid, use a fork to lightly pierce the skin over the breast, and brush with the paprika mix. Now lock the crisping lid, reset the unit to the Air Crisp cooking mode at 200ºC and set the time to thirty mins. Press START/STOP to start.
6. When it's over, (The intern temp should be 75ºC) pull the cooked duck out of the unit and give it a rest of ten mins before serving.

### Cooking & Prep Time: 1 hr 5 mins

Servings: 4

# KOREAN CHICKEN WINGS

## Ingredients

- 30g Light brown sugar
- Salt & pepper
- 15ml of olive oil
- 1kg of frozen chicken wings

**For the sauce:**
- 30ml tamari soy sauce
- A tsp of chilli flakes
- Two garlic cloves, minced
- 60ml honey
- 1cm of grated ginger
- 15ml of sesame oil
- 50g Gochujang paste
- Zest & juice of a 1/2 lime
- 5ml of Apple Cider Vinegar

## Directions

1. In the beginning, pour a cup of water into the pot of your Ninja foodi machine, add the crisping basket inside and place chicken wings on it, Close the lid and Select Pressure on Hight, set time to ten mins and press START/STOP to start.
2. During the cooking process, combine the rest of the components in a pan and heat up over medium, stirring. When it starts bubbling, decrease the heat and simmer for about three to five mins. Remove the saucepan from the heat and leave it aside warm.
3. When the machine has completed the cooking time, quick release the steam. Open the lid and grease the wings with olive oil and season with salt & pepper. Reset the unit to the Air Crisp cooking mode and set the time to ten minutes, Press START/STOP to begin, checking the internal temp has reached 76ºC.
4. Coat the wings in the prepared sauce, and garnish using sesame seeds & spring onions If you want!

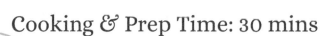

### Cooking & Prep Time: 30 mins

### Servings: 4

# CRISPY DUCK BREAST

## Ingredients

- 100g green lentils
- Two duck breasts with skin
- 100g pickled beetroot, diced
- A handful of spinach and rocket salad
- 240ml of vegetable stock
- A tsp fresh coriander, chopped
- 400ml hot water
- Salt & pepper

**Beetroot Vinaigrette:**

- 5ml of balsamic vinegar
- 25ml pickled beetroot juice
- 35ml rapeseed oil
- 10g honey
- 3g of mustard

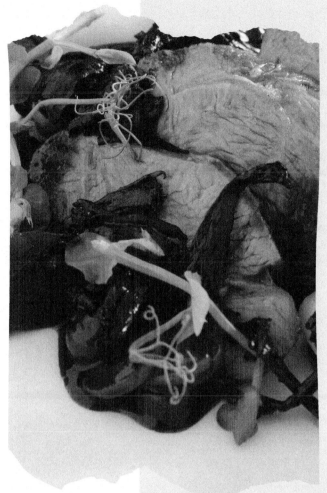

## Directions

1. Place the lentils in the pot of your Ninja Foodi Unit, and pour the stock and water over. Close the pressure lid, (the valve in the SEAL). Set the Unit to the PRESSURE cooking mode on Hight, and set the time to three mins. Press START/STOP to start.
2. When it's completed, set the valve to the VENT to quick release the pressure. Remove the lentils and drain them, Wash out the pot and put it back in the Unit.
3. Reset the Unit to the SEAR/SAUTÉ cooking mode on MEDIUM and preheat for five mins. During the cooking time, score the skin of the duck without cutting the meat and then use some salt & pepper to season it on all sides.
4. Put the prepared breast skin down into the pot without oil and sauté on each side for three mins.
5. Then pull the breast out of the pot, discard all excess fat and insert the reversible rack in the high position. Put the duck breasts on the rack skin side up, luck the lid and choose AIR CRISP, at 200ºC and set the time to ten mins. START/STOP.
6. At the same time, combine the warm lentils with beetroot, and coriander in a bowl, and add salt & pepper to season if needed.
7. When the time is over, pull the cooked breasts out of the machine and give it a rest of ten mins. During that, mix the components that are listed in the "Beetroot Vinaigrette" section in a bowl and whisk them together until emulsified, It takes around two to three mins.
8. Present the spinach & rocket with the prepared vinaigrette and serve with the sliced breast & lentils.

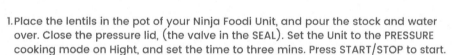

## Cooking & Prep Time: 39 mins

### Servings: 2

# CHICKEN SOUP RECIPE

## Ingredients

- A whole chicken
- A leek
- A litre of water
- peppercorns
- celery root
- Three carrots
- Two onions
- One piece of ginger
- Two bay leaves
- Two parsley stems
- A parsnip
- 1-2 garlic cloves
- chilli powder

## Directions

1. In the first step, peel the parsnip, celery root, leek, and onion and cut them into big pieces. Then place them with all the other listed components except for the carrots & spices in the pot of your Ninja Foodi.
2. Close the lid and set the unit on the Pressure cooking function on Hight, the release valve should be in SEAL position. Set the time to forty mins. Press START/STOP to start.
3. When the time is over, quick release the pressure by shifting the valve to the VENT.
4. Open the lid, remove the chicken and cut it into tiny pieces, season the stock with salt & pepper, Chilli and parsley. Add carrot slices and place them with the pulled chicken again into the pot.
5. Simmer the mixture for an additional few mins, and serve the soup with fresh herbs and noodles, or of your choice.

Cooking & Prep Time: 1 hour

Servings: 2

19

# MOROCCAN-STYLE CHICKEN RECIPE

## Ingredients

- A whole chicken
- A tsp of cumin
- A half-pickled lemon
- Handful green olives
- A tsp of turmeric
- Ten saffron strings
- A tbsp of fresh parsley
- Four garlic cloves
- Two to three white onions
- A tsp of ginger
- salt & pepper
- A tbsp of fresh coriander
- 60ml of olive oil

## Directions

1. Turn on the Ninja Multi-Cooker Unit and set it on the SEAR/SAUTE cooking mode, add 15ml of oil, place the chicken in the pot and roast on both sides.
2. Chop the onions, herbs and garlic, add them to the chicken in the pot and keep cooking for a further five mins.
3. Then add all the listed spices & lemon. Change the cooking mode in your Ninja Foodi to PRESSURE mode on HIGH and set the time to forty mins.
4. When it's over, remove the pressure lid and change the cooking mode this time to AIR FRY and cook for thirty mins.
5. Transfer to a serving platter and serve with fries and bread.

Cooking & Prep Time: 1 hr 30 mins

Servings: 2

# MEAT

Homemade British Cooking

# LAMB CURRY RECIPE

## Ingredients

- 30ml of Oil
- Salt
- A large Onion, diced
- One and a half tsp of crushed ginger
- A tsp of Green Chilli, crushed
- A half tsp of Turmeric Powder
- 60ml Water
- A tsp of Cumin Powder
- 400g tinned Tomatoes, pureed
- A tsp of Coriander Powder
- One and a half tsp garlic, crushed
- 900g of diced Lamb
- A half tsp of Red Chilli Powder
- A tsp of Garam Masala Powder
- Two Peeled Potatoes, cut into quarters
- 500g Water

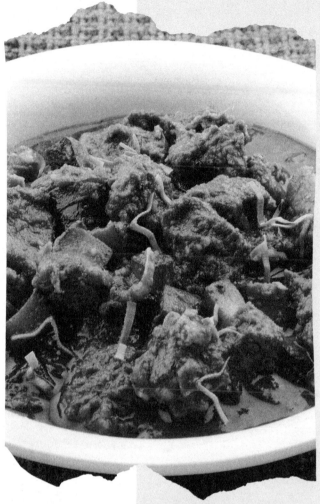

## Directions

1. In the beginning, set the Unit to the SEAR/SAUTÉ cooking mode, pour oil and add Garlic, Onions, Green Chilli, and Ginger, sauté for around eight to ten mins, then add the lamb and sera for two to three mins.
2. Pour 60ml Water over to deglaze the pot and then add all the other mentioned ingredients. Close the pressure lid, Choose PRESSURE mode, and set the time to twenty-five mins. Press START/STOP to start.
3. After the cooking time is completed, shift the valve to the VENT to release the pressure quickly. Check if the meat is cooked, and add Potatoes, stir through. Close the pressure lid, Choose PRESSURE on Hight, and set the time to five mins. Press START/STOP to start.
4. When the cooking process is over, shift the valve to the VENT to release the pressure quickly. If you like the sauce to be thicker, sauté without covering until you get the desired thickness.

### Cooking & Prep Time: 45 mins

### Servings: 6

# TASTY TONKOTSU BEEF BELLY RAMEN RECIPE

MEAT RECIPE

## Ingredients

**For the broth:**
- 1.5kg Beef bones
- Two carrots, roughly chopped
- A celery stick roughly chopped
- A quartered onion
- Five chestnut mushrooms, halved
- Two spring onions, halved
- Four garlic cloves, peeled
- 1-inch sliced garlic
- Two bay leaves
- 30g of miso paste
- Two sachets dashi
- Salt

**For the beef belly:**
- Salt & pepper
- 1kg of beef belly, skin on

**For the toppings:**
- Two pak choi
- 100g enoki mushrooms
- 300g ramen noodles
- Three diagonally sliced spring onions
- A red chilli, thinly sliced
- Sesame seeds
- Four eggs, soft-boiled
- Seaweed

## Directions

1. First, you will start by boiling the beef bones for five mins, then rinse them well. Set the Ninja Foodi Unit to the SEAR/SAUTÉ cooking mode on High. Press START/STOP, add all the listed aromatics except for teh bay leaves and brown them. Add the beef bones over, pour water to cover and then add the bay leaves. cook on High for sixty mins. When it's finished, let the pressure release naturally for fifteen mins.
2. Strain the broth into a suitable pot using a cheesecloth-lined colander, then add miso paste & dashi and whisk them together. Season with salt, remove any fat that appears on top and place over low heat.
3. At the same time, season your beef belly using salt & pepper and score the skin in a diamond pattern. Cook in your oven for thirty mins at 230ºC, then decrease the heat to 140ºC and keep cooking for fifty mins. Let it cool down before slicing.
4. Cut off the end of the pak choi, then quickly boil it to blanch for two mins, and put it in ice water. Cook the ramen noodles following the packet directions, and stir fry the enoki mushrooms briefly with a pinch of salt & sesame oil.
5. Transfer to serving bowls, top with sesame seeds and serve!

### Cooking & Prep Time: 2 hours

Servings: 4

22

# DELICIOUS NAVRIN OF LAMB RECIPE

## Ingredients

- 2kg shoulder of lamb, off the bone, cut into 4cm cubes
- A large onion, finely sliced
- Two cloves of garlic, crushed
- One bouquet garni
- 100g baby carrots
- 15ml of oil
- 200g small new potatoes
- 15g of tomato puree
- 250g sliced leeks
- Four small turnips, halved
- 300ml Apple Juice
- Salt & freshly ground pepper
- One large bay leaf
- 350ml lamb stock
- 100g green beans

## Directions

1. In the beginning, set the Unit to the SEAR/SAUTÉ cooking mode on High. Press START/STOP to start. Pour oil and heat it for around two mins. Add 1/2 of lamb to the pot, and cook on all sides until it becomes brown. Remove it and cook the remaining lamb the same way. Remove it and drain off all but a tbsp of fat in the pot.
2. Now, add the chopped onion and cook for about two mins. Then add potatoes, baby carrots, garlic, leeks, and turnips to the pot and cook for five to six mins till they become soft. Add the precooked lamb with juices again to the pot. pour apple juice, stock, tomato purée, green beans, herbs, and season!
3. Close the lid, and put the pressure release valve in the SEAL. Set the Unit to the PRESSURE cooking mode on HIGH. Set the time to thirty-five mins. Press START/STOP to start cooking.
4. Quick release the pressure after the cooking process is done, pull the pot out and serve hot with vegetables.

Cooking & Prep Time: 1 hr 20 mins

Servings: 4

23

# AWESOME GRILLED LAMB CHOPS & RICE PILAF

## Ingredients

**For the pilaf:**
- Three garlic cloves, crushed & peeled
- An onion, diced
- Juice and zest from one orange
- 100g pomegranate seeds
- 500ml of chicken stock
- 50g toasted almonds, roughly chopped

- 10g each parsley, mint, and fresh dill chopped roughly

**For the lamb:**
- Olive oil to brush
- Twelve fresh lamb chops
- Salt & pepper
- Pomegranate syrup
- Salt & pepper
- 400g basmati rice, well rinsed

## Directions

1. In the beginning, set the Unit to the SEAR/SAUTÉ cooking mode Medium-High and preheat for five mins. Then pour oil in the pot, add onions and sauté for about five to eight mins. Then, add garlic and cook for an additional min. Finally, add stock along with rice.
2. Lock the pressure lid, (the valve in the SEAL). Reset the unit to the PRESSURE Cooking mode on Hight, and set the time to two mins. Press START/STOP to start.
3. After completing the cooking time, let the pressure release for ten mins naturally, then shift the valve to the VENT to quick release the pressure.
4. Fluff rice and add the remaining listed components, cover and put it aside. Wipe out the pot and put it back in the Ninja Foodi Unit. Insert the reversible rack (in the lower steam position, without top tier ) into the pot.
5. Now, use the olive oil to brush the meat and season on both sides. Then, arrange six chops on the rack.
6. And now, seal the crisping lid, set the Ninja unit to the GRILL cooking function and set the time to seven mins. Press START/STOP to start.
7. After three min of cooking, flip the chops. Next, install the top tier and put the rest of the chops on it. When they are cooked and get your desired looking, transfer them to a plate and cover them loosely with foil to rest before serving. Transfer them to a serving plate with pilaf, drizzle with Pomegranate syrup and serve.

## Cooking & Prep Time: 45 mins

### Servings: 6

24

# MINTY LAMB RECIPE

## Ingredients

- Three cloves of garlic
- A half leg of lamb, (raw) around 1.2kg
- 20ml vegetable oil
- 25g thickening gravy granules
- Salt & freshly ground black pepper
- 25g finely sliced fresh mint

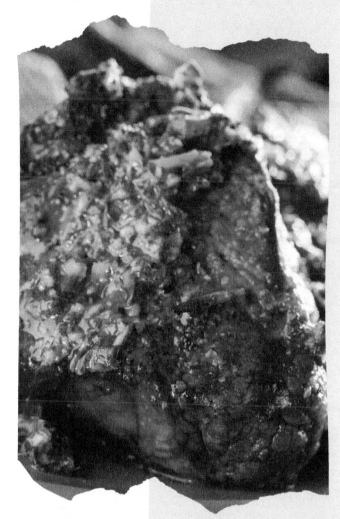

## Directions

1. In the beginning, the lamb on your working board, and puncture the meat all around using a sharp knife to make short slits in the meat. Insert the garlic slices in those slits and season with ground black pepper & salt
2. Inside the pot of the Ninja Foodi unit, add 200ml cold water, put the prepared meat into the Cook & Crisp Basket and then put it into the pot. Lock the pressure lid, (the valve in the SEAL). Set the unit to the PRESSURE cooking mode on Hight, and set the time to thirty-two mins. Press START/STOP to start.
3. When the cooking process is completed, let the pressure release for two mins naturally, then shift the valve to the VENT to quick release the pressure.
4. Now, unlock the lid and brush the lamb with vegetable oil, Close the crisping lid, choose AIR CRISP mode at 200ºC and set the time to eight mins. Press START/STOP to start. When it's completed, pull the basket out of the machine and give the lamb a rest covered in aluminium foil.
5. Add the gravy granules to the cooking liquid in the pot, stir to combine, and pour more water if needed. Close the pressure lid, (the valve in the SEAL). Select PRESSURE on LOW, and set the time to three mins. Press START/STOP to start.
6. After the cooking time is completed, shift the valve to the VENT to quick release the pressure. Open the lid and adjust the consistency of the sauce as desired and stir. Transfer it to a suitable bowl and add the mint slices.
7. Put the cooked leg meat on a platter for serving, and pour the sauce over to coat.

Cooking & Prep Time: 1 hr 55 mins

Servings: 6

# AWESOME MEATBALL PASTA BAKE

## Ingredients

- 100g grated mozzarella
- 250ml water
- 50g parmesan cheese, grated
- 680g beef mince
- 250ml Cranberry Juice
- 60ml milk
- 45g seasoned breadcrumbs
- 15g fresh parsley, chopped
- Two large eggs
- Two tsp of Sea salt
- 45ml of olive oil
- Two tsp of granulated garlic
- 450g dry cavatappi pasta
- 1.36kg marinara sauce
- 250g ricotta cheese

## Directions

1. In the first step, crack the eggs in a large bowl, and add parmesan cheese, beef mince, bread crumbs, milk, garlic, parsley, and salt. Mix them well together to combine and then, shape twenty balls of this blend.
2. Next, set the Ninja Foodi Unit to the SEAR/SAUTÉ cooking mode on High. Press START/STOP to start preheating for five mins. Then pour oil into the pot, arrange ten balls and brown them on all sides. Remove them and repeat with the rest ten balls.
3. Add the water along with the marinara sauce, Cranberry or Red Grape Juice into the pot and add the pasta; stirring to incorporate.
4. Lock the lid, and put the pressure release valve in the SEAL. Reset the unit to the PRESSURE cooking function on LOW. Set the time to two mins. Press START/STOP to start cooking.
5. When the cooking time is completed, let the pressure release for ten mins naturally, then shift the valve to the VENT position to quick release the pressure. Open the lid.
6. Again, reset the cooking function and this time to the SEAR/SAUTÉ mode on MD. Press START/STOP to start, stir and then add the ten balls, simmer for ten mins. Decrease the temperature if the sauce comes to a boil.
7. Now, add the ricotta and top the whole mix with mozzarella. Change the cooking function to BAKE/ROAST at 160ºC, and set the time to five mins, or until cheese is melted & slightly browned. Serve it right away!

### Cooking & Prep Time: 40 mins

Servings: 10

# DELICIOUS BEEF AND RED CABBAGE RECIPE

## Ingredients

- 450g sliced beef stew meat
- 120g sour cream
- A red cabbage head, shredded
- 30ml essential organic olive oil
- A red onion, chopped
- Salt & black pepper

## Directions

1. In the beginning, set the Ninja Foodi unit to the SEAR/SAUTÉ cooking function on your Ninja Foodi, pour oil, heat it up, add the onion, and also the meat, and brown for five mins.
2. Then add the rest of the listed components, Lock the lid and put the pressure release valve in the SEAL. Reset the unit to the PRESSURE cooking mode on High. Set the time to twenty mins. Press START/STOP to start cooking.
3. Release pressure naturally for ten mins, divide the mixture into serving bowls and serve.

Cooking & Prep Time: 30 mins

Servings: 4

# GOAT AND SWEET ONION

## Ingredients

- Three chopped sweet onions
- Salt & black pepper
- 680g sliced goat tenderloin
- 120ml beef stock
- 15ml extra virgin olive oil

## Directions

1. Choose the SEAR/SAUTÉ mode on your Ninja Foodi, pour oil, heat it up, and add the onions and sauté for five mins. Add the goat tenderloin and the remaining ingredients, Close the lid and put the pressure release valve in the SEAL. Choose PRESSURE on High. Set the time to twenty-five mins. Press START/STOP to start cooking.
2. Release pressure to have success naturally for ten mins, transfer to serving and serve.

Cooking & Prep Time: 35 mins

Servings: 4

# AWESOME MAPLE CHOPS

**MEAT RECIPE**

## Ingredients

- 450g lamb chops
- 90g maple syrup
- 15ml essential olive oil
- Two garlic cloves, minced

## Directions

1. Mix all the listed components in a wide bowl and toss to coat the chops.
2. Transfer the chops to the basket of your Ninja Foodi and insert the basket into the machine. Lock the crisping lid, set the unit to the AIR CRISP cooking mode at 195ºC and set the time to twenty mins. Press START/STOP to start.
3. When the crisping process is completed, pull the basket out of the machine. Transfer everything to platters and serve.

Cooking & Prep Time: 30 mins

Servings: 4

# BEEF BRISKET RECIPE

MEAT RECIPE

## Ingredients

- 1kg beef brisket
- 300ml beef stock
- Beef or BBQ seasoning

## Directions

1. As a first step, place the Beef in your chosen seasoning and let it marinate for at least one hr in the fridge, When it's marinaded, transfer the beef to your Ninja Foodi and add the Stock over it.
2. Lock the pressure lid, (the valve in the SEAL). Set the Ninja Foodi unit on the PRESSURE cooking function on Hight, and set the time to sixty mins. Press START/STOP to start. When it's over, let the compression release for two mins naturally, then set the valve to the VENT to quick release the pressure. Open the lid and pull the Beef out of the machine and let it take a rest for fifteen mins.
3. Change the cooking function on the Unit to the Sauté mode (High) and reduce the Juices until you get the desired consistency. After that, Shred the Brisket until it falls apart.
4. Add over your beef juices reduction and serve with sides of your choice.

### Cooking & Prep Time: 3 hours

Servings: 4

30

# SIDES

# HONEY GLAZED PARSNIPS

## Ingredients

- 250ml water
- 15g of sunflower oil
- 30g of runny honey
- A tsp fresh thyme leaves
- 500g parsnips
- 2g of sea salt flakes

## Directions

1. In the beginning, peel the parsnips and cut them into quarters or eights if large. Put parsnips into the Basket of your Ninja Foodi Multi-cooker unit, and insert the basket into the pot with water.
2. Close the lid and put the pressure release valve in the SEAL. Choose PRESSURE on HIGH. Set the time to zero min. Press START/STOP to start cooking. When the cooking time is over, shift the valve to the VENT position to quick release the pressure. Open the lid, and remove the water. Leave the parsnips squash to steam dry for five mines.
3. Combine the rest of listed components the in a bowl, and brush the parsnips with it the mixture to coat.
4. Close the crisping lid, set the unit to the AIR CRISP cooking function at 200°C and set the time to fifteen mins. Press START/STOP to start. Flip and cook for an additional five mins if needed. Serve immediately!

### Cooking & Prep Time: 30 mins

Servings: 4

31

# DELICIOUS CREAMY MASH

## Ingredients

- 90g of butter + more for serving
- 125ml water
- 900g of potatoes
- 5g of salt
- A half tsp of black pepper
- A tbsp of herbs of your choice
- 125ml-200ml cream

## Directions

1. After peeling the potatoes, add them to the pot of your Ninja Foodi and pour water over to cover.
2. Lock the lid and put the pressure release valve in the SEAL. Set the unit to the PRESSURE cooking mode on HIGH. Set the time to twelve mins. Press START/STOP to start cooking. When the cooking time is over, shift the valve to the VENT to quick release the pressure.
3. Then unlock the lid and use your masher to mash the potatoes, then add the butter along with black pepper, cream and salt till you get your desired consistency.
4. Finally, add the chosen herbs and mix everything to combine.

**Cooking & Prep Time:** 20 mins

Servings: 4

32

# CRANBERRY & ORANGE SAUCE

## Ingredients

- Zest & juice from a large orange (You can use more)
- 100g Light brown sugar, soft
- 250g frozen cranberries

## Directions

1. In the beginning, set the Ninja Foodi unit to the SEAR/SAUTÉ cooking function on MD: HI, add orange and sugar and press START/STOP to begin. When the combine starts boiling in about four mins, let it boil until it becomes slightly thickened.
2. Add the cranberries and decrease the temperature to LO: MD, simmer for seven to ten mins until the cranberries are cooked without losing their form. Stir a few times while cooking. Let it cool down.
3. Preserve the sauce in an air-tight container and place the container in the fridge to stay for a week or so.

Cooking & Prep Time: 25 mins

Servings: 4

# SPINACH GRATIN SIDE DISH

SIDE RECIPE

## Ingredients

- 400ml whole milk
- 800g baby spinach
- 30g of butter
- 15ml of olive oil
- 100g grated gruyère cheese
- A chopped onion
- Two garlic cloves, crushed
- A half tsp of nutmeg, freshly grated
- Two tbsp of plain flour
- 45g of parmesan cheese, grated
- salt & pepper
- 20g of breadcrumbs

## Directions

1. In the beginning, set the Ninja Foodi unit to the SEAR/SAUTÉ cooking function and set it to MD: HI, add olive oil and butter to melt in the pot, then add onion and cook for around ten mins. Add garlic and cook for a further ten mins.
2. Decrease the heat to MD, add flour, mix and cook for a couple of mins creating a roux. While stirring, pour the milk into the roux slowly to combine it with the roux which will become smooth. Add nutmeg along with salt & pepper.
3. Gradually, add the spinach while stirring to combine and wilt. Press START/STOP, and stir gruyère into the spinach. add parmesan & breadcrumbs over the spinach mixture.
4. Lock the crisping lid and set the Ninja unit to GRILL, set the time to six mins. Check spinach browning after four mins and serve right away!

Cooking & Prep Time: 35 mins

Servings: 6

34

# ROASTED BUTTERNUT SQUASH WITH SAGE & CHILLI

## Ingredients

- 250ml water
- 15ml of olive oil
- 1kg butternut squash
- Three fresh sage leaves, chopped
- Sea salt flakes
- A half tsp of chilli flakes

## Directions

1. Start with cutting the butternut squash into quarters or eights if it's large. Then place it into the Cook & Crisp Basket of your Ninja Foodi, and insert it into the pot with water.
2. Lock the lid and shift the pressure release valve to the SEAL position. Set the unit to the PRESSURE cooking function on High. and set the time to zero mins. Press START/STOP to start cooking. When the pressure process is completed, let the pressure release for ten mins naturally, then set the valve to the VENT to quick release the pressure. Unlock the lid, and remove the water. Leave the butternut squash to steam dry for five mines.
3. Combine the sage leaves with chilli flakes, oil, and salt in a bowl, mix and use them to brush butternut squash until it's fully coated.
4. Close the crisping lid, reset the unit to the AIR CRISP cooking mode at 200ºC and set the time to fifteen mins. Press START/STOP to start. Flip and cook for an additional five mins if needed.
5. When the time is over, pull the basket out of the unit. Transfer everything serving platters and serve right away.

### Cooking & Prep Time: 30 mins

Servings: 4

35

# CHILLI HASSELBACK RECIPE

SIDE RECIPE

## Ingredients

- 30ml of olive oil
- A tsp lemon zest
- 800g small potatoes, prepared for Hasselback
- Juice of one lemon
- Salt & pepper
- A half tsp of chilli flakes

## Directions

1. In a mixing bowl, mix the zest or sumac, with olive oil, chilli flakes, lemon juice, salt & pepper and mix well.
2. Add the basket inside the Ninja Foodi unit, lock the lid, set the unit to the ROAST cooking function at 200ºC and set the time to thirty mins. Press START/STOP to start preheating.
3. When the unit is preheated (It beeps), add the potatoes into the basket inside and brush with the chilli mixture. Lock the lid.
4. In the middle of the cooking time, unlock the lid and brush potatoes with the chilli mixture another time, Lock again and keep cooking until the time ends. Serve them right away!

### Cooking & Prep Time: 45 mins

### Servings: 4

# POTATO CHIPS

## Ingredients

- Five Large Potatoes, peeled, sliced into thick chips
- Salt
- 30 to 45ml of Oil
- Vinegar

## Directions

1. First, you will start by soaking the Potatoes in a bowl of water for ten mins, then drain, rinse them and pat dry with a towel. Now put the potatoes into the basket of the Ninja Foodi in a single layer and pour oil over them.
2. Toss to coat and season and close the crisping lid. Set teh unit to the AIR CRISP cooking function at 180ºC and set the time to twenty mins. Press START/STOP to start.
3. When it's completed, check if the potatoes are cooked, and cook for a further five mins or more if needed.

Cooking & Prep Time: 35 mins

Servings: 6

# CAULIFLOWER CHEESE RECIPE

## Ingredients

- A medium head of cauliflower, cut into florets
- 500ml whole milk
- 50g plain flour
- Salt & freshly ground black pepper
- 5g of dried English mustard powder
- 100g of mature cheddar cheese, grated
- 250ml water
- 50g cubed unsalted butter

## Directions

1. In the pot of your Ninja Foodi, add the cauliflower florets and pour water over them. lock the lid and put the pressure release valve in the SEAL. Choose PRESSURE on LOW. Set the time to one min. Press START/STOP to start cooking. When the pressure process is completed, shift the valve to the VENT position to quick release the pressure.
2. Unlock the lid, and place the cooked cauliflower in a colander to drain. Wipe out the pot and put it back in the machine.
3. Change the cooking mode of the unit to the SEAR/SAUTÉ and set it to MD HI, Press START/STOP, pour milk and add flour with butter to the pot and whisk them until they become thick with a silicone balloon whisk. Then, Decrease the temp to low medium.
4. Add mustard along with 1/2 cheese and seasoning, whisk again, add the drained cauliflower and top with the rest of the cheese.
5. Now, lock the crisping lid, Set the unit to the AIR CRISP cooking function at 200°C and set the time to seven mins. Press START/STOP to start. The cheese should be golden brown when the cooking ends. Enjoy!

## Cooking & Prep Time: 22 mins

### Servings: 4

# SAGE & ONION BALLS

## Ingredients

- A large onion, peeled & finely chopped
- Zest from a lemon
- 50g pine nuts
- 25g butter
- A garlic clove, peeled and crushed
- 100g fresh breadcrumbs
- Three tbsp of fresh finely chopped sage leaves
- Salt & pepper
- A beaten egg

## Directions

1. First, set the Ninja Foodi unit to the SEAR/SAUTÉ cooking function and set it to HI, Press START/STOP to preheat for five mins.
2. add pine nuts to the pot, then add onion and toast for about two mins until they become lightly brown. Then remove them from the pot.
3. Keeping the unit in the SEAR/SAUTÉ mode, set it to LO: MD and press START/STOP to run. Add butter to melt it. then garlic & onion, cook for twenty mins. Stir occasionally. Let the mix cool for ten mins.
4. Now, transfer it to a medium bowl and mix the rest of the mentioned components. Grease your Ninja multi-purpose tin. Put the mixture in the tin and pat it down into an even layer. Lock the crisping lid. Reset the unit to the BAKE/ROAST cooking function at 100ºC, and set time the to twenty to twenty-five or until golden brown.

Cooking & Prep Time: 1 hours

Servings: 4

# TASTY SPICY BEEF JERKY SIDE DISH RECIPE

## Ingredients

- 200g flank steak – cut into 2mm thick slices
- A half tsp of chilli flakes
- 2g of salt
- A half tsp of cayenne pepper

## Directions

1. Combine all the listed components in a suitable bowl. Spread the steak slices on your chopping board and pound out a little bit. The steak should become around 1mm thin.
2. Add the pot and put the reversible rack into the lower position. put 1/2 of the meat on the rack and then add the top tier. Add the remaining meat and lock the crisping lid. Set your Ninja Foodi unit to the DEHYDRATE cooking mode and set the time to eight hrs. Press START/STOP to start. Store the cooked meat in an airtight container for about a week or so.

Cooking & Prep Time: 18 mins

Servings: 4

40

# FISH & SEAFOOD

Homemade British Cooking

# Chapter: 5

# AWESOME PRAWN FRY RECIPE

## Ingredients

- 30ml of Coconut Oil
- A tsp of Mustard Seeds
- 5g of Ginger Paste
- A diced onion
- Ten fresh Curry Leaves
- 450g Deveined King Prawns, Without shell
- 5g of Garlic Paste
- 3/4 tsp of Red Chilli Powder
- A half tsp of Turmeric Powder
- 45ml of Water
- 15ml of Lemon Juice
- A quarter tsp of ground Black Pepper
- Two tbsp of fresh chopped Coriander

## Directions

1. First, set the Ninja Foodi unit to the SEAR/SAUTÉ cooking function and preheat it with oil. Add Mustard Seeds and follow with Onions, Garlic Paste. Sauté for five mins, Then add the Curry Leaves and after ten seconds add the Prawns along with the remaining ingredients except for the Coriander & Lemon Juice and cook for two mins.
2. Lock the lid and set the unit to the PRESSURE cooking mode on HI. Set the time to four mins. Press START/STOP to start cooking. When the time is over, shift the valve to the VENT to quick release the pressure.
3. Drizzle the Lemon Juice on top and garnish with the Coriander.

Cooking & Prep Time: 20 mins

Servings: 4

# DELICIOUS SALMON PIE

## Ingredients

- 1kg peeled potatoes, cut into 2cm chunks
- 500g skinless salmon, cubed (3cm)
- 150ml fish stock
- 250ml water
- 70ml milk
- A half tsp of salt
- 150g broccoli, cut to small florets
- 50g butter
- 150ml single cream
- 50g butter
- A medium onion, peeled & chopped
- 50g plain flour
- 350ml milk
- freshly ground black pepper
- 200g cooked prawns, peeled
- 7g of fresh parsley
- 50g Gruyere cheese, grated
- Cooking Spray

## Directions

1. Add the potatoes to the pot of your Ninja Foodi machine and pour water over them. Lock the lid and set the unit to the PRESSURE cooking mode on HIGH. Set time to seven mins. Press START/STOP to start.
2. When the time ends & pressure release is done, unlock the lid, drain the potatoes if they are not already, place them in a large bowl and mash with a half tsp of salt, pepper, milk, and butter; and cover to keep warm. Wipe out the pot and put it back in the unit.
3. Set the unit to the SEAR/SAUTÉ cooking mode on the 4th level. Press START/STOP to heat up the Ninja Foodi for a couple of mins, then melt the butter in it, add onion and sauté for five to seven mins, stirring occasionally.
4. Add flour and sauté for an additional minute. Gradually pour the fish stock, and milk and add cream making sure that it's not lumpy, cook for a few mins until it starts to thicken.
5. Now, add the broccoli, and change the cooking mode to the SEAR/SAUTÉ to the 3rd level. Cook for a few mins, then decrease the heat to 2nd level and add salmon, parsley, and prawns, season to taste and simmer for a few additional mins. Then, add the mashed potatoes mixture over all, and top with the grated cheese.
6. Close the lid and reset the unit to the AIR FRY cooking function. press ROAST/BAKE at 170ºC and set the timer to twenty mins. Press START/STOP to start.
7. When it's completed, the pie would become golden brown.

### Cooking & Prep Time: 8 mins

### Servings: 2

# TOMATO MUSSELS

## Ingredients

- 1kg whole mussels
- 15ml of oil
- Two cloves of garlic, peeled & minced
- 300ml fish stock
- Two shallots, peeled & finely chopped
- 300g tomatoes, roughly chopped
- Fresh chopped parsley for serving
- Two tbsp of chopped fresh flat-leaf parsley
- Salt & freshly ground black pepper
- 15ml of lemon juice
- 25g butter

## Directions

1. As a first step, wash the mussels with water and discard any debris that sticks to the shell. Set your Ninja Foodi unit to SEAR/SAUTÉ cooking mode on HI. Press START/STOP and preheat for five mins.
2. Then pour oil into the pot, add shallots and garlic and sauté for three mins. Then pour the fish stock over and cook for a further five mins
3. When the stock has reduced, add parsley, mussels, tomatoes, and season with salt & pepper.
4. Lock the crisping lid, set the unit to the ROAST/BAKE cooking function at 180°C and set the time to ten mins. Press START/STOP to start.
5. Once it's done, add the lemon juice along with butter to melt it. Top with fresh herbs and serve immediately!

Cooking & Prep Time: 38 mins

Servings: 2

43

# TASTY SALMON RECIPE

## Ingredients

- 15ml of lemon juice
- A teaspoon of red chilli powder
- Two pieces salmon
- Half teaspoon turmeric powder
- A teaspoon of ginger, crushed
- 15ml of oil
- Half teaspoon garam masala
- Three garlic cloves
- Pinch Salt

## Directions

1. First, you will begin with drying the salmon fillets using a paper towel, then add oil and rub on both sides of the fillets, then continue rubbing the salmon fillets with all other mentioned ingredients.
2. Turn on your Ninja Unit, insert the Air Frying basket and place the prepared salmon fillets into it.
3. Lock the lid, set the unit to the AIR FRY cooking function at 200°C and set the time to five to six mins. Press START/STOP to start.
4. When it's over, check the fillets cook for more time if it's needed.

Cooking & Prep Time: 10 mins

Servings: 2

# MUSTARD COD WITH BEANS AND BEEF BACON

## Ingredients

- Three garlic cloves, peeled and minced
- 500g green beans
- 115g Dijon mustard
- 125ml double cream
- A bunch of fresh tarragon, minced
- 5g of sea salt
- Half tsp of black pepper
- Four cod fillets (115g each)
- 200g beef bacon, cut into 1cm pieces
- A medium white onion, peeled, diced and divided
- 125ml water

## Directions

1. Combine teh tarragon, cream, mustard, garlic, 1/2 onion and salt & pepper in a bowl, mix them and add cod fillets and toss to coat. Put the bowl in the refrigerator to marinate for one to four hours.
2. Set the Ninja Foodi Unit to the SEAR/SAUTÉ cooking function on HIGH. Press START/STOP to heat up the unit for a couple of mins, then add the beef and cook for around five to seven mins, stirring occasionally, until it becomes crispy and fat. Then add the remaining half onion and keep cooking for a further couple mins, stirring often.
3. Now, add the beans with water to the pot and stir to combine, Lock the lid and set the unit to the PRESSURE cooking mode on LO. Set time to zero mins. Press START/STOP to start.
4. When the cooking time ends, shift the valve to the VENT position to quick release the pressure.
5. After the pressure release is done, open the lid, Put the marinated cod fillets in the MultiPurpose pan. Place it over the rack and insert the rack in the close position to be over the green bean mixture.
6. Close the lid and set the unit on the ROAST/BAKE cooking function at 160°C and set the timer to fifteen mins. Press START/STOP to start.
7. Make sure to check the doneness after twelve mins, and stop the cooking once the internal temp is 65°C, and the cod fillets start browning. Serve immediately!

### Cooking & Prep Time: 4 h 45 mins

Servings: 4

45

# GOAN FISH CURRY

## Ingredients

**For the curry:**
- A peeled clove from a small bulb of garlic
- 35g root ginger, peeled
- Two-star anise
- 30ml of coconut oil (melted)
- One and a half tsp of ground cumin
- 30ml of apple cider vinegar
- 30ml of water
- A tbsp of mild curry powder
- A tbsp of ground coriander
- A tsp of ground turmeric
- 2g of sea salt
- A quarter tsp of ground red chilli powder
- One and a half tsp of black mustard seeds
- A diced onion
- A quarter tsp of ground cloves
- Two tbsp of coconut sugar
- A large tomato, diced
- 30ml of lime juice
- 400ml tinned coconut milk
- 600g cubed cod loin or pollock, sprinkled with sea salt
- 3/4 cup fresh roughly chopped coriander

**For the Tarka:**
- Handful curry leaves
- 45ml of coconut oil
- A tbsp of black mustard seeds

## Directions

1. Set the Ninja Foodi Unit to the SEAR/SAUTÉ cooking function, set it on LO:MD, and press START/STOP to start preheating the cooking pot. Then add the stars and dry roast until fragrant, then transfer them to your bullet blender and add coconut oil, garlic, apple cider vinegar, ginger, water, coconut oil, and remaining spices except for the mustard seeds, Blend everything well to produce a paste.
2. Put your prepared paste in the pot, and add the mustard seeds over, fry for around three mins while stirring, then add onion and fry for an additional three to five mins. Add the rest of the mentioned components except for the coriander & fish and reset the temp to MD. Simmer for five mins.
3. Now, add the fish, Close the lid and put the pressure release valve in the SEAL. Set the unit to the PRESSURE cooking mode on LO. Set the time to three mins. Press START/STOP to start cooking. When the cooking time ends, shift the valve to the VENT to quick release the pressure.
4. Pull the pot out of the Unit and let it cool down for around five mins before stirring in the coriander. Add the lime juice & extra sea salt to taste.
5. During that, let's make the Tarka, Melt the coconut oil in a non-stick pan, and add black mustard seeds, and curry leaves. Cook until the seeds start popping, add it over the curry when served.

**Cooking & Prep Time: 21 mins**

**Servings: 4**

# UK STYLE SALMON RECIPE

## Ingredients

- 30ml of Olive Oil
- Half tsp of Smoked Paprika
- Two Salmon Fillets, dried (115g each)
- A tsp of your desired dry Herbs
- 1.5g of Salt
- A quarter tsp of Black Pepper

## Directions

1. In a bowl, mix salt, smoked paprika, pepper and olive oil, and put the fish fillets into the bowl and coat it with this mixture on both sides.
2. Arrange the fish fillets on the Cook & Crisp Basket, and add the Basket to the preheated Ninja Foodi.
3. Close the lid, and set the unit to the AIR FRY cooking function at 200℃, set the timer to eight mins and press START/STOP to start.

### Cooking & Prep Time: 8 mins

### Servings: 2

# NINJA FOODI SHRIMP RISOTTO RECIPE

## Ingredients

- 25g of grated Parmesan cheese, + more for serving
- 30ml of olive oil
- A small onion; peeled, finely diced
- A tsp of ground black pepper
- Four peeled & minced garlic cloves
- 15g of Sea salt
- 1.37L vegetable stock

- 16 uncooked jumbo prawns, peeled & deveined
- Two tsp of garlic powder
- 400g Arborio rice
- 30g of butter
- Juice from one lemon
- A trimmed asparagus bunch, cut into pieces

## Directions

1. Choose the SEAR/SAUTÉ mode, MD:HI on your Ninja Foodi, and press START/STOP to start preheating for five mins. Pour 15ml of oil into the pot, add onion and sauté for around five mins. Add 1/2 of garlic and cook for a further min. Add 10g of salt to season.
2. Now add the rice and pour the stock over, Close the lid and put the pressure release valve in the SEAL. Choose PRESSURE on HIGH. Set the time to seven mins. Press START/STOP to start cooking.
3. At the same time, add the prawns to a bowl, pour the rest of the oil, and add black pepper, salt, garlic powder, and garlic. Toss to coat.
4. When the cooking time ends, let the pressure release for ten mins naturally, then shift the valve to the VENT position to quick release the pressure. Open the lid, add asparagus along with the lemon juice and stir to combine.
5. Put the reversible rack into the pot over the risotto, (in the higher position). Transfer the prepared prawns to the rack. Lock the crisping lid, choose GRILL mode and set the time to eight mins. Press START/STOP to start.
6. When the grilling time ends, pull the rack out of the machine, add the parmesan to the risotto and stir, then add the prawns over and top with more parmesan and serve immediately!

### Cooking & Prep Time: 50 mins

Servings: 6

# TASTY PRAWN CURRY

## Ingredients

- 200g Tomatoes Pureed, tinned or fresh
- A tsp of Red Chilli Powder
- 12g Ginger Paste
- 45ml of Vegetable Oil
- A diced Onion
- A tsp of Garam Masala Powder
- 5g of Garlic Paste
- 30g of Tomato Puree
- A tsp of Coriander Powder
- 1/2 tsp Turmeric Powder
- 200g King Prawns Cleaned & Deveined
- A tsp of Madras Curry Powder
- 5g of Green Chilli Paste
- 30ml of Water
- One and a half tsp of Cumin Powder

## Directions

1. Set the Ninja Foodi unit to the SEAR/SAUTÉ cooking function, and press START/STOP to heat it up. Add and heat up the oil, then add Garlic & Onion and saute for around five mins. Add the Green Chilli with Garlic and sauté for a further min.
2. Add the Tomato Puree & Tomatoes and stir, Then add the rest of the components, and finish with water and Prawns.
3. Lock the lid and set the unit to the PRESSURE cooking mode on HI. Set the time to five mins. Press START/STOP to start cooking. When the process is completed, shift the valve to the VENT to quick release the pressure. Serve!

### Cooking & Prep Time: 10 mins

Servings: 4

# EASY FISH FRY IN THE FOODI

## Ingredients

- Two Fillets of your favourite white Fish; cut into chunks
- 3/4 tsp of Red Chilli Powder
- A tsp of Cumin Powder
- A tsp of Coriander Powder
- A quarter tsp of Turmeric Powder
- Half tsp of Paprika
- Salt & Pepper
- Three tbsp of Cornflour
- Half tsp of Garlic Powder
- Cooking Spray

## Directions

1. Mix all the listed components except for the fish in a shallow dish and mix them well together.
2. Place the fish chunks into the mix, toss and rub well to coat. Transfer the fillets to the Cook & Crisp Basket, add the Basket inside the preheated Ninja Foodi unit, and spray with cooking spray.
3. Close the lid, and set the unit to the AIR FRY cooking mode at 200°C, set the timer to eight mins and press START/STOP to start.
4. When it's completed, flip the fillets and air fry for an additional three to four mins. Enjoy!

Cooking & Prep Time: 15 mins

Servings: 2

50

# DESSERTS

# QUICK CHERRIES CREAM

## Ingredients

- 5g vanilla flavouring
- 350g Double cream
- 450g pitted cherries
- 60g white sugar

## Directions

1. In your Food Processor, combine all of the components, and divide the mixture into four ramekins.
2. Insert the reversible rack inside the Foodi, squeeze ramekins inside, set the unit on the Baking cooking function, and cook at 150ºC for a quarter-hour. Serve this cream cold.

Cooking & Prep Time: 30 mins

Servings: 4

# COFFEE CHOCOLATE CAKE

## Ingredients

- Four eggs
- Handful chocolate glazed coffee beans
- A pack of Bicarbonate of soda (baking soda)
- A tbsp of vanilla flavour
- 240ml of cold coffee
- 240g of butter
- 210g of flour
- 600g of sugar
- 3/4 cup of chocolate glaze
- 60g cacao powder

## Directions

1. In the beginning, you will start with cooking the coffee, then leave it to cool down completely. Mix the vanilla flavour, butter, and sugar in a bowl using a mixing device. Add eggs and combine.
2. Combine the bicarbonate of soda with flour in a separate bowl and add cacao powder to them.
3. Gradually, add the flour mix and cold coffee to the dough and mix everything to combine.
4. Transfer the dough to a ring cake baking tin and put it into the pot of your Ninja Foodi unit. Set the unit to the BAKE cooking mode and set the temperature to 170ºC and the time to forty mins. Serve it cold!

Cooking & Prep Time: 1 hour

Servings: 8

# YUMMY CHEESECAKE GLASS

## Ingredients

- 40g melted butter
- Lemon abrasion
- Two eggs
- Frozen berries for the topping
- 150g cream cheese
- 80g spoon biscuit
- 1/2 vanilla pulp
- 30g Light brown sugar
- 10g starch
- 300g skimmed quark
- Red groats

## Directions

1. In the beginning, start with crushing the biscuits and mixing them with melted butter. Transfer the mixture to four jars and press it firmly.
2. Combine the cream cheese, quark, starch and sugar in a mixing bowl, and mix well. Scrape out the pulp of the vanilla pod and add to the cheese mix. Add the eggs with lemon abrasion, mix and spread the mixture evenly on the bottom over the biscuits mix.
3. Add a wide bowl of water inside under the Ninja Foodi grid, and arrange the jars on the grid. Lock the lid. Set the unit to the BAKE cooking mode, at 175° C and cook for around thirty-five to forty minutes. Remove and allow to cool.
4. Let the jars cool down, Add the red groats over, top with frozen berries and serve.

Cooking & Prep Time: 45 mins

Servings: 4

# AWESOME CREAM CHEESE PUDDING DESSERT

## Ingredients

- Two whisked eggs
- 30g sugar
- 450g soft cream cheese
- 10g melted butter
- 250g melted chocolate brown

## Directions

1. Mix all the mentioned ingredients in a wide bowl, whisk well and divide the mixture between four ramekins.
2. Insert the reversible rack into Ninja Foodi, place the ramekins into it, and set the unit to the Baking cooking function, cook at 170ºC for 20 mins and serve cold.

Cooking & Prep Time: 25 mins

Servings: 4

# CREAMY GRAPEFRUIT

## Ingredients

- One whisked egg
- 250g coconut cream
- 30g sugar
- 60ml grapefruit juice

## Directions

1. Mix all the mentioned ingredients in a wide bowl, whisk well and transfer the mixture to a ramekin.
2. Insert the reversible rack inside Ninja Foodi, place the ramekin into it, and set the unit to the Baking cooking function, cook at 160°C for 15 mins. Divide into cups and serve cold.

Cooking & Prep Time: 20 mins

Servings: 6

# SIMPLE PEACH UPSIDE-DOWN CAKE IN THE FOODI

## Ingredients

- 12g of Baking Powder
- Three sliced and skin removed Peaches
- 75g Butter
- One egg
- 150g Light Brown Sugar
- 60g of Butter
- 180g Plain Flour
- 160g Milk
- A quarter tsp of Nutmeg
- Pinch of Salt
- A tsp of Ground Cinnamon
- 100g Light Brown Sugar

## Directions

1. In the beginning, grease a seven-inch cake tin with butter.
2. Set your Ninja Foodi unit to the SEAR/SAUTÉ cooking mode, and melt butter with sugar on it. Arrange the peach slices on the prepared tin.
3. Whisk the butter mix for five mins in your stand mixer. Then add milk with the egg and whisk again to combine. Stir in the flour, salt, baking powder, nutmeg and cinnamon.
4. Pour the mixture over the peach slices into the greased tin.
5. Insert the trivet into the machine and place the tin covered with foil on it.
6. Lock the lid and shift the pressure release valve to the SEAL position. Set the unit to the PRESSURE cooking function on Hight. Set the time to twenty mins. Press START/STOP to start cooking. When the time ends, let the pressure release naturally for ten mins.

Cooking & Prep Time: 30 mins

Servings: 8

56

# EASY BANANA CAKE RECIPE

## Ingredients

- 200g golden caster sugar
- 3g of salt
- A tsp of baking powder
- 100ml sunflower oil
- A tsp of mixed spice
- Two ripe bananas, with skins on
- Two large eggs
- 200g self-raising flour

## Directions

1. Grease the loaf tin of your Ninja Foodi Unit, and then line round it.
2. Place all the listed components in your Food Processor and mix them together until you get a smooth dough and transfer it to the prepared loaf tin.
3. Set the unit to the BAKE/ROAST cooking function at 160°C on your Ninja Foodi, and press START/STOP to start preheating for five mins. Then put the tin into the pot. Reset the unit to the BAKE/ROAST cooking function, at 170°C and cook for fifty to sixty mins. (In case the cake starts browning much fastly, cover it with aluminium foil)
4. Check the cake by inserting a wooden toothpick. Enjoy!

Cooking & Prep Time:  1 h 10 mins

Servings:  8

# CLASSIC GREEK CAKE RECIPE

## Ingredients

- 240g soft Greek yoghurt
- 5g baking powder
- Two whisked eggs
- 50g white sugar
- 120g white flour
- 3g vanilla flavouring
- 30g melted butter
- Cooking spray

## Directions

1. Whisk all the ingredients in a bowl except the cooking spray.
2. Add the reversible rack inside Foodi, add a cake pan inside and grease it using the cooking spray.
3. Transfer the blend to the pan and cook it on the Baking function at 180°C for a half-hour. Cool down, slice, and serve.

Cooking & Prep Time: 36 mins

Servings: 8

58

# TASTY RED VELVET CHOCOLATE RECIPE

## Ingredients

- Two tins of full-fat coconut milk, 400g each (free from gums/additives)
- A quarter tsp of nutmeg
- 500ml beetroot juice
- 200g roughly chopped dark chocolate
- 60ml maple syrup
- Zest & juice of 1 orange
- Three cinnamon sticks
- 15ml of vanilla extract
- 5ml of orange extract
- A quarter of tsp of ground cloves
- A tsp of ground ginger
- Pinch sea salt

## Directions

1. Add all the listed ingredients to the cooking pot of your Ninja Foodi Unit and gently stir with a spoon.
2. Lock the lid and put the pressure release valve in the SEAL. Set the unit to the PRESSURE cooking function on LOW. Set the time to five mins. Press START/STOP to start cooking.
3. When the cooking time ends, shift the valve to the VENT position to quick release the pressure. Unlock the lid, stir and transfer to serving glasses.
4. Serve them cold with your desired toppings.

Cooking & Prep Time: 7 mins

Servings: 8

# MOIST CHOCOLATE CAKE

## Ingredients

**For the base:**
- 240g of soft butter
- Three tbsp of Bicarbonate of soda (baking soda)
- 140g of sugar
- A pack of vanilla sugar
- 200g sour cream
- 125g of flour
- Pinch salt
- 25g of cacao powder
- Three eggs
- 60ml of milk
- 100g grated dark chocolate

**For the frosting:**
- 150g chocolate glaze
- 100g cream

## Directions

1. Combine the vanilla sugar with butter and sugar in a bowl using a mixing device. Add eggs gradually, then the sour cream and mix again.
2. In a separate bowl, combine the cacao powder, flour, bicarbonate of soda, and salt. Add this to the dough you've made in the previous step. Then pour milk over, add dark chocolate and mix everything to combine.
3. Place the whole dough in the pot of your Ninja Foodi and set it to the BAKE cooking mode for forty-five mins, then test with a skewer and allow it to cool down.
4. Chop the chocolate and put it in a bowl, boil up the cream in a pot, and add it over the grated chocolate glaze, Whisk them well to melt and combine and spread it over the cake.

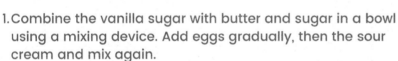

### Cooking & Prep Time: 1 hour

Servings: 8